ALSO BY BERNIE KEATING:

PIVOT TO ASIA

A New U.S. Foreign Policy?

In a new focus to its foreign policy, the United States will attempt to place a greater emphasis on relationships with Asian nations and the region of the pacific.

BERNIE KEATING

authorHOUSE®

AuthorHouse™
1663 Liberty Drive
Bloomington, IN 47403
www.authorhouse.com
Phone: 1 (800) 839-8640

Published by AuthorHouse 06/28/2017

ISBN: 978-1-5246-9792-1 (sc)
ISBN: 978-1-5246-9793-8 (hc)
ISBN: 978-1-5246-9791-4 (e)

Table of Contents

PREFACE

This book has gone through a labored journey.

The initial draft was completed two years ago when President Obama announced his Pivot to Asia and placed greater emphasis on things in the Pacific, but tentative changes occurred in the President Trump administration with uncertainty about the Pivot.

Then followed some ambiguity by the author about the premise and conclusions; so, that took considerable more analysis and re-writing.

Finally, after reexamining the role of my own changing rationales, I wondered if I really wanted to be so revealing about my own private religious beliefs – too personal.

When publishing a new book, I no longer think I am building another pyramid; I am not so naïve or humble. Yet, the words placed on paper have meaning to me, even if to no one else.

Bernie Keating

A PIVOT TO ASIA

The Foreign Affairs policies of the United States are flexible from one administration to another as a consequence of the thinking of the President, but also as a result of the reaction to intervening events.

In recognition of the emergence of China as a major concern in Asia, President Obama announced a *pivot* in our nation's Foreign Affairs policy to place a new emphasis on events in the pacific. This came with a realization that countries in Asia play an important role in our nation's future security and economy. The pivot was announced late in his term in office and it remains to be seen if it will be a priority with other presidents; however, the importance of Asia in the affairs of the world is a reality that cannot be ignored.

A nation's Foreign Affairs policy is also a product of the religious beliefs of a nation. Our culture developed in the United States as a result of the Judeo-Christian religious ethos we inherited from Europe. Our early ancestors carried their religious beliefs with them across the Atlantic, oblivious to atheistic religions in the Pacific as if they did not exist; hence, our American culture is actually a European culture.

As a consequence, because of our ignorance about Asia, we have been ill-equipped to deal with that region. Mistakes include isolation from Japan in the 1930's, the Vietnam War and Korean War fought unsuccessfully to prevent communist aggression, the optional Iraq and Afghanistan War, ambivalent relations with Pakistan and India, and quarrels with China. Do we know enough about Asia and Asians to react correctly to future developments?

We will start this pursuit with a look at our religious legacy because it represents our most fundamental beliefs and the one that creates a unique "state of mind" that impacts with our political and economic cultures.

2

AN ALMIGHTY GOD?

The religion we inherited from Europe that a monotheistic, almighty God controls our universe was a regrettable legacy from our European ancestors. It led us into worshiping a fictional creation. There is no almighty God that is the fundamental belief of each of the three major religions of the world that originated in the West: Judaism, Christianity, and Islam. The religion, Christianity, is a made-up creation; as a consequence, we have been led to worship a myth. Yes, Christianity is a myth. [1]

Wow! That is a strong statement: an almighty God that controls the universe does not exist? That assertion will cause some people to catch-their-breath, suck in air, and exhale slowly. They will quarrel with the statement; likely to feel it is an exaggeration. Most likely, it will be met with: "who the hell is he to say that?" A creation myth was a normal human evolution. As the night's darkness fell over the European countryside, man trembled in fear of unknown dangers in the darkness and superstitions. With the new day's light, they felt reverence and fell to their knees – some spirit has seen them safely through the darkness. It is little

---

[1] Myth: "A widely held but false belief or idea", Oxford Dictionaries

7

wonder that man embraced an almighty God for security and thanksgiving for his care. [2]

By contrast, the Asian man required only the assurances of his tribal elders to make it through the night, accepting the privations and difficult challenges of survival. The western populations of one half of the world required belief in an almighty God; the other Asian half needed only the security of his Buddhist enlightment or the rituals of his Hindu ancestry traditions.

Each of the three western religions began as a cult. [3] They fit the classic definition of how a new religion begins, but most such neophyte religions never progress beyond this initial phase and eventually die a natural death. Each of these religions, Islam, Christianity, and Islam, then audaciously embellished their legends in a long chaotic process of religious dogmata. [4] All three of these religions believe in the supernatural as a tenant of their faith; so, they could

---

[2] "A creation story is a cultural, traditional or religious myth which describes the earliest beginnings of the present world. Creation myths are the most common form of myth, usually developing first in oral traditions, and are found throughout human culture." Wikipedia, 2017

[3] Cult: "a religion regarded as unorthodox or spurious," *Webster's New Collegiate Dictionary*.

[4] Legend: "Story coming down from the past regarded as historical although not verifiable", Webster's New Collegiate Dictionary, Merriam-Webster, MA, 1977.

have based their religious faith on that, but instead attempted to create a legend in an unbelievable mix of fact and fiction.

Many smart people were taken-in and worshiped in the wrong pew for centuries – including Popes, philosophers, bishops, Rabi, scholars, perhaps even my Mother and Dad – and so was I during my childhood and for many decades as an adult. But somewhere along the line some of my doubts began to surface. Our inherited belief in an almighty God does not make us narrow-minded or bigoted; we mostly had no other choice; it was the religious hand we were dealt.

Yet, half of the people in the world were among the unbelievers – they were not taken in. A majority of the people in our universe do not believe in a monotheistic, controlling God. They are atheist - yes, a majority of the world's population is atheist.

What has this to do with a pivot to Asia in the Foreign Affairs policy of the United States? Actually quite a bit; but I am ahead of myself, so let me start anew.

The constitution of the United States is a document that stipulates the internal workings of our nation and its people. It does not look outward at relationships beyond its borders except to specify how to make

Declarations of War. What was clearly stated in our constitution by our founding fathers was that we were a nation "under God." A Foreign Affairs policy for our nation is not addressed in the constitution. As a consequence, our nation's follow-up has always been reactive to events at the time. Here is an outline of priorities during the early decades of our nation's history.

> *Post-Revolutionary War:* the early priority was defense against Great Britain and for good reason; inasmuch that the British invaded portions of the new republic and even set fire to the White House.
>
> *Pre-Civil War:* the nation was preoccupied internally with issues of states' rights and slavery.
>
> *Post-Civil War:* the nation's priority became internal westward expansion.
>
> *Sea Power policy* dominated for a century. An American Naval officer, Alfred Mahan, was the chief proponent of a strong navy to defend our shores against foreign powers.

World War One: this was the first Foreign Affairs policy of consequence when President Wilson led American Forces to Europe to fight against the threat from Kaiser Wilhelm and Germany.

Post-World War One: the focus of American Foreign Affairs policy turned inward in isolation from the rest of the world.

Pearl Harbor: this was a wake-up call when our nation was forced to re-engage with the rest of the world during World War Two. Following the end of the war, the American Marshall Plan helped rebuild Europe.

Cold War: The United States led the establishment of NATO and the European Common Market in support of a containment policy. Two American Security Advisers during the Cold War, Henry Kissinger and Zbigniew Brzezinski, are credited with focusing our policy on "Eurasia", (Russia) the central zone of Asia that stretches from Asia Minor to Japan.

Henry Kissinger, who was Secretary of State under President Nixon, wrote in his book *Diplomacy*: "The United States must maintain the global balance of power vis-à-vis Russia with its long history of expansionism." [5] Zbigniew Brzezinski, who was National Security Advisor under President Carter, launched his book *The Grand Chessboard* several years later. His book described the American triumph in the Cold War in terms of control over Eurasia: "… all have agreed that who rules Eurasia, rules the world." [6]

The containment of Russia, a Foreign Affairs policy from the 1950's, continues to be a central focus of our nation's policy to the present day.

---

[5] Kissinger, *Diplomacy,* 1994,New York, Simon & Shuster, p. 814

[6] Zbignew, *The Grand Chessboard*, 1997, Perseus Books, NY, p Xiii

OUR BIASED RELIGIOUS HERITAGE

Politics and economics do not exist in a vacuum; they occur with a "state of mind" created by religion; hence, religious philosophy is the starting point to understand the motives of populations relative to their political rationales and economic realities. Religious beliefs create the cultural climate within which they operate.

The past failure of the Americans to understand Asians is because of the Judeo-Christian bias we inherited from our European forefathers. Our symbol, "In-God-we-trust", is meaningless to the Buddhist, Hindu, Sikh, and other aesthetic cultures of Asia. Therein lays a problem with our foreign affairs: we and Asians dance to dissimilar philosophical tunes.

As Christians we function with a different "state of mind" from people in Asia. [7] While we look outward to our almighty God, Asians with their Buddhist, Hindu, and Atheist heritages look inward within their self or at their godless cultures. They have no almighty God who controls their universe and tells them what to do. These Asian non-spiritual convictions are incompatible with our "pie-in-the-

---

[7] "State of Mind: The status of one's consciousness, their perception of the outside world, their mood or temperament, and perception of their own circumstance", Wikipedia, 2016

sky" beliefs that came from Europe. We demand a role for morality in government, i.e. "the Christian Golden Rule"; whereas, Asians take an irreligious, pragmatic, and secular approach to their politics.

This dichotomy is illustrated by the allegiance required by every American schoolboy: "one nation, *under God*, with liberty and justice for all"; whereas, no nation in Asia claims to be *under God*. The song *God Bless America* has become virtually an American national anthem.

The current globalization concept now in vogue has saddled Western nations with a further religious penalty. The metaphor of a flat world with a level playing field places a restraint on us with our religious ethics; whereas, Asians are not similarly constrained. We worry about a moral code; they do not.

Historically, our culture has this religious bias because our heritage comes from Europe. Our Christian religion and culture are European based; we cut our teeth at home and in school learning what flowed from across the Atlantic as if what lay on the other side of the Pacific did not exist. If we are to understand these differences, we must understand the state-of-mind of other populations, and that will inevitably lead us to the subject of religion. [8]

---

[8] "State of Mind", op. cit.

We failed in the past to understand that Asian populations differ in religious culture from American people with our Judaic-Christian prejudice; consequently, they have a different "state-of-mind." Religiously, America and Asian nations are poles apart. This problematic religious milieu also creates differences in motivation toward politics and economics.

The definition of a religion is a belief in a God or some other philosophy that relates people with each other. Even though most people in the West believe in a monotheistic God, a majority of the religious in Asia does not; most are atheists, Buddhists, Hindus, or believe in some other atheistic or cultural concept.

Defining the word "religion" is fraught with difficulty. Many focus on a narrow definition that matches their own religion but include few others. All definitions contain at least one difficulty; they exclude beliefs of practices that many people passionately defend as religious; for example, their definition of religion might require a belief in a God who is responsible for creation of the universe, but that excludes such non-theists religions as Buddhism and Hinduism, the two dominant religions of Asia.

Here are the religious world statistics in 2016. [9]

Religion	# Adherents	% of World Population
Christian	2.2 billion	31.5
Muslim	1.6	22.3
Non-religious	1.1	15.4
Hindu	1.0	13.9
Buddhist	376	5.3
Chinese	394	5.5
Traditional	300	4.2
Sikh	23	0.3
Jewish	1.4	0.2
Other	131	1.8
TOTAL:	7.2 billion	

Religion is a discriminating factor in East-West relations because of our Judeo-Christian belief in a monotheistic God. Buddhism is the predominate culture of the East, often in synergy with religions such as Taoism and folk religions in China and Japan; Hindus dominate India; Sunni Muslims are the majority in Indonesia and Pakistan; Shia Muslims dominate Iran, and some Christians are in Asia as a result of proselyting by missionaries or colonists.

[9] "Statistics of Religion", Wikipedia, 2016

These variants in religious concepts affect how people approach politics. In America there is a Judeo-Christian political bias with a particular emphasis on morality that is absent in Asia. Our concept of Christian morality is politically irrelevant to most nations and populations in Asia.

WESTERN RELIGIONS

Christianity is an monotheistic religion based on the life and teachings of Jesus Christ. Christians believe that Jesus is the Son of God and the savior of humanity whose coming as the Messiah was prophesied in the Old Testament, and has played a prominent role in the shaping of Western civilization. [10]

Judaism is an ancient monotheistic Abrahamic religion and encompasses the religion, philosophy, culture and way of life of the Jewish people. [11]

Islam is an Abrahamic monotheistic religion that professes that there is only one and incomparable God (Allah) and that Muhammad is the last messenger of God. [12]

---

[10] "Christianity", Wikipedia, 2017

[11] "Judaism", Wikipedia, 2017

[12] "Islam", Wikipedia, 2017

Abrahamic religions are religions that share the patriarch Abraham in their lineage, although he plays different roles in different belief systems. [13]

Atheism is the absence of belief in the existence of deities. [14]

---

[13] "Abrahamic", Wikipedia, 2017
[14] "Atheism", Wikipedia, 2017

IS THERE AN
ALMIGHNTY GOD?

I began in with the statement that there is no almighty God, which is the fundamental belief of each of the three western monotheistic religions: Judaism, Christianity, and Islam. What was my basis for making such a claim? You may challenge that statement and it is my responsibility to explain how I arrived at that conclusion.

It is not a new assertion. In *Searching for God,* my book published in 2013, I undertook a rigorous examination of this subject and utilized my academic education as a physicist. [15] I intended it to be more than just a token search looking for a god-like entity but a serious look by a reasonably unbiased person. I explored all the possible theories for the existence of an Almighty God.

I began with an investigation of the theories for the origin of the universe, which included the following:

> Creation as related in Genesis 1:1-1:2
>
> Big Bang Theory
>
> Creationism
>
> Steady State Theory
>
> Chaotic State Theory
>
> Multiverse Theory

---

[15] Bernie Keating, *Searching for God,* Authorhouse 2013

Pantheism

After a thorough examination, I concluded that none of these theories for the origin of the universe have convincing, factual evidence for the existence of a God; however, none of them excluded the possibility that the supernatural is an option.

I then looked at the universe from another perspective. It behaves in a manner that follows a set of existing physical laws: gravitation, electromagnetism, the strong force, and the weak force. None of these physical laws lent themselves to a belief in a God.

I continued the search among the subatomic particles that create all the matter in the universe, such things as atoms, molecules, electrons, quarks, leptons, bosoms, dark energy and dark matter, and the all the newly identified elements of quantum theory. This examination ruled out the possibility that a God was somehow nestled in among these elemental subatomic particles.

After completing this rigorous investigation, I reached the following conclusion:

Is there a God?

> Yes, there may be if you believe in the supernatural.

<u>No</u>, there is no almighty God that exists
in the scientific (natural) world.

Since I do not believe in the supernatural, I do not believe in the existence of an almighty God.

Before we begin a discussion of other religions, we must start with an understanding of our own personal roots. Let me review mine; let me admit to my own lifelong bias. This will come as no surprise to anyone who read my 2013 book, *Searching for God*.

My father was Catholic, and I was raised in the religious faith of my father. My Mother was raised as a Methodist and did not convert to becoming a Catholic until twenty five years after marriage, when I was an adult and away at college. She always attended Sunday Mass and supported the religious beliefs of the rest the family, but on those other three Sundays when the missionary priest did not come to Buffalo Gap; she took us to the Methodist church where I learned the Saint James bible. I was an altar boy, was married in the church, and met all the criteria as a "practicing" Catholic. As recently as a couple years ago I was a Eucharistic Minister at Mass and distributed communion to Catholic parishioners.

During the 1960s shortly after Vatican Two, our family participated in home Masses that were encouraged at that time. We found them to be much more in the tradition of the early church where the Mass was thought of as a "meal and prayer" celebration among friends and family. We loved the cultural traditions that the home Mass created among our circle of friends that included a couple priests, a nun, a doctor, and several other families; The experience helped to provide for a much deeper "quality-of-life" experience than simply going to a church building. Then home Masses fell out of favor in the post-Vatican Catholic Church so we returned to the prior tradition in a parish church.

Although I do not believe in the monotheistic God of the Christian church, I am a promoter of the rich culture created by the Christian church. I have visited almost every cathedral in Europe. They are an impressive historical display of our Christian culture; unfortunately they are now almost empty except for tourist. Christianity is a dying concept throughout many European populations and atheists are the majority.

A person must distinguish between his own Christian belief, which is a futile search, and the Christian culture, which is a rich experience. We should continue to embrace our Christian culture.

Until recent years I did accept the existence of a God and had no reason or motivation to challenge the belief; it was not a popular thing to do. In American social circles, atheists are often considered uncivilized and only a step removed from a heathen. I do not know when my belief changed, but I think it occurred when I did the research and wrote my book in 2013. With a background in physics, I began a very deliberate search through all the known science, looking for any evidence for the existence of a God. I explored the existing theories about the origins, and all the physical laws that govern our universe. After completing a thorough search, I concluded the following:

"I did not find any evidence for a God, except possibly in the supernatural; however, we are not alone if we reach out and embrace the cultural traditions that add substance to our lives."

Since I have never believed in the supernatural, I do not believe in a God; you can't convince yourself to accept something that you do not believe. I am comfortable in my belief as an atheist. I have never made any pronouncement about my religious faith to anyone, and do not think it is the business of anyone else.

There, I completed that personal religious discussion; so, let me proceed with the rest of the book.

RELIGIOUS PHILOSOPHIES
IN THE WEST

The differences in religious philosophies can be traced to two icons of history: Socrates in the West, who created the concept that man has a *"soul"*; and Gautama (Buddha) in the East, who stressed that a man must look inward within himself seeking *"enlightenment"*. [16] We look outward to an almighty God and the Asian religions look inward. Each of these concepts of Socrates and Gautama evolved during the muddled process of history to the more complex religions and dogmas of today. "It was Socrates who created the conception of the soul, which has ever since dominated European thinking." [17]

Let's briefly look at the major religions that originated in the West or Middle East: Judaism, Christianity, and Islam. All three are monotheistic (belief in one God). All three began as cults within other religions of their

---

[16] *"Enlightenment: In Buddhism, enlightenment meant ceasing to be preoccupied with one's personal condition and attainment and to devote oneself to helping and teaching others; finally, a realization that true enlightenment is a matter of endless practice and compassionate functioning, not something that occurs once and for all in one great moment"*, Wikipedia, 2016

[17] A.E. Taylor, *"Socrates: the Man and his Thought,"* Doubleday Anchor book, published 1933 in England, and 1952 in America, pg. 132

time. Each persisted as legends for decades before becoming self-identified as a religion. [18] [19]

JUDAISM:

The Judaic religion had its roots in a Semite tribe in ancient Mesopotamia in 2000 BCE when a man named Terah took his son, Abraham and family, from the city of Ur in Babylon and migrated six hundred miles north into the region now called Turkey. According to their legend, the God *Jehovah* gave him a covenant: "If Abraham will follow the commandments of God, his descendants will become God's chosen people." This ancient legend became the foundation of the Judaic Religion. During the early centuries of their existence, the Hebrew was a nomadic tribe that trekked through the deserts of the Middle East, Egypt, and finally settled in Judea; "A fundamentally scattered nature of Jewry even from the beginning." [20] As the religion evolved during the following centuries of dispersal, its code (called the Talmud) was crystalized into a body of knowledge: first by a Moroccan named Alfasi; another

---

[18] Cult: "a religion regarded as unorthodox or spurious," *Webster's New Collegiate Dictionary*.

[19] Legend: "Story coming down from the past regarded as historical although not verifiable", Webster's New Collegiate Dictionary.

[20] H.G. Wells, *The outline of History*, Garden City Books, Vol One, p. 417

by a North African, Maimonides; and finally a third revision in 1665 CE by Joseph Cargo in Jerusalem. [21]

Today, the Judaic religion has various sects including Orthodox, Reform, Conservative, and Hasidic. [22]

CHRISTIANITY:

The Christian religion began in Jerusalem as an outgrowth of the Judaic religion when a Jewish rabbi named *Jesus* began to preach and attract large crowds of followers. The disciples of this enigmatic, mysterious man called him a God and created a cult within the Roman occupation. [23] The people were impressed by his grandeur, awed by his moral supremacy and mysteriousness, kept in reverence by his closeness to God, and attracted to him by his kindness and humility. [24]

The foundation dogma of the Christian religion was not established until three centuries later in AD 325 at Nicaea, a town in the region of Turkey, where a

---

[21] Rabbi Joseph Telushkin, Jewish Literacy, William Morrow, N.Y., 2001, p. 11

[22] Religious Sect: is a subgroup of a religious or philosophical belief system, usually an offset of a larger group, that breaks away to follow a different set of rules and principles.

[23] Cult: "a religion regarded as unorthodox or spurious," *Webster's New Collegiate Dictionary.*

[24] Wells, op. cit. p. 528

conference of early Christians came together under the leadership of the Roman Emperor Constantine to organize and agree on a common doctrine called the Nicene Creed. This became the credo of all Christians. In his book, *Crossing the Threshold of Hope*, Pope John Paul stated: "the words of the Nicene Creed is nothing other than the reflection of Saint Paul's doctrine." [25]

During the following centuries, the Christian church splintered into sects including Roman Catholic, Eastern Orthodox and Protestant. The Christian sacred book is the Bible.

ISLAM:

This religion originated decades after the Christian religion in the sixth century. The founder, Muhammad, was an Arab boy who led camel caravans across the deserts from Yemen through Arabia to Syria. During his travels through Syria, he encountered people of the Christian faith and wondered why his Arab tribes had no similar religious faith. [26] According to legend,

---

[25] Paul ll, Pope John Paul, *Crossing the Threshold of Hope*, Alfred A Knopf, 1994, p. 46
[26] Wells, op. cit.

the God *Allah* manifested himself in the form of the Angel Gabriel to Muhammad. [27]

A splintering apart of Islam started after Muhammad's death in the tenth century. The sect known as "Sunnis" chose Abu Behr, Muhammad's closest companion, as leader. The sect known as "Shiites" supported the claim of Ali Bin Abi Toleb, Mohammad's, son-in-law, to become the caliph (or leader). The Sunnis, recognized by many as the traditional Islamic religion, today represents a majority of all Muslims. Except for Iran, their religion is nearly world-wide. Their sacred book is the Koran. [28]

In opposition to these three religions are atheists who deny the existence of God. They are the majority in Scandinavia, Germany, Netherlands, China, and elsewhere. According to recent polls, fifteen to twenty percent of people in the United States are non-religious or atheist. [29] The number of atheists is on the rise across the world with religiosity generally declining. [30]

---

[27] "Mohammed", *Colliers Encyclopedia*, op. cit., p. 284

[28] Keating, *Riding the Fence lines*, op. cit., p. 116

[29] "Non-religious in the U.S," Wikipedia, 2016

[30] "Demographics of Atheism", Wikipedia, 2016

MAJOR ASIAN RELIGIONS

The dominate religions in Asia are Buddhist, Hindu, Sikh, and Islam.

There is little commonality among Asian religions; they originated at different times and in different ways, but none have the same philosophies as the three monotheistic religions that originated in the West and Middle East.

Buddhism is the predominate religion of Asia often in synergy with other religions; Hinduism dominates India; Sunni Muslims dominate Indonesia and Pakistan, Shia Muslims dominate Iran; China is atheistic but with some folk religions; and Christians are scattered as a result of proselyting. None except Islam looks outward to a monotheistic God. That leads to a different state-of-mind of their populations than that held by most Americans.

Let me now provide a brief look at a few major Asian religions I have personally encountered during my travels.

Buddhism: a religion originated in India by Gautama Buddha five centuries before Christ that later spread to Afghanistan, Burma, Tibet, China, Japan, and other parts of Southeast Asia. It no longer exists in India, the home of its birth. A Buddhist believes that life is full of suffering caused by desire and that the way to end this suffering is through *enlightenment.* [31]

My first encounter with Buddhism was in Japan, where it is called Shinto. An important development in my education came many years later when my oldest daughter became an AFS exchange student and lived with a Buddhist family in Thailand. She loved her family there and remains in contact now 50 years later.

Today, Buddhism is the dominate religion of Asia, but under different names and often in synergy with other religious philosophies. There are an estimated 400 million Buddhist worldwide. [32] Buddhism allows devotees to incorporate elements of other religions into their individual practice. [33]

Hindu: is the world's third largest religion (behind Christianity and Islam) and is the majority in India. Hinduism contains a broad range of philosophies and is a synthesis of various Indian traditions with diverse roots and no founder. Practices include rituals such as: worship, recitations, meditation, family rites of passage, annual festivals, and occasional pilgrimages. [34]

---

[31] "Buddhism", *Encarta 97 Encyclopedia*, Microsoft 1997

[32] "Buddhism", *Colliers Encyclopedia*, op cit., p. 21

[33] *Modesto Bee*, Dennis Robins, Staff writer, 4/14/96

[34] "Hinduism", Wikipedia, 2016

From a Western standpoint it is referred to as a religion, but in India the term dharma is preferred, which is broader than the western term religion. [35]

Hindu presence in the United States was virtually non-existent before the passage of the Immigration and Nationality Services Act of 1965, which opened up the opportunity for more immigrants from the Eastern Hemisphere. Hindus from India account for more than 2 million in the United States; they hold the highest education levels among all religious communities in the United States and many are computer experts employed in Silicon Valley. [36]

Two of my children live and work in Silicon Valley with Hindu as neighbors and classmates in their children's schools. It brings a new and broadening element into the American culture.

Sikh: My first encounter with a Sikh was a fellow alumnus who was participating with me on a project for our alma mater, University of California, Berkeley. He was an engineering graduate who worked as a scientist in Silicon Valley. There are many Sikh such as him working there.

---

[35] Ibid

[36] "Hindus in America", *Wikipedia*, op cit.

The complex polyglot nature of Sikhism makes it almost uncommunicable to Westerners. The concept of God is mystical in character and the ideas concerning life after death are vague. It may be considered something racial, religious, or communal, and sometimes merely a movement. [37]

The Sikh religion arose in the 15th century at the time of the Mughal Empire. The Mughal emperors claimed direct descent from Genghis Khan, who ruled a couple centuries earlier.

Canada has a large number of Sikh with 2% of the population. There are fewer in the United States, but the current American Ambassador to the United Nations and former governor of South Carolina, Mikki Haley was born and raised a Sikh.

ISLAM: this was discussed in a previous chapter. It originated in Arabia so is not considered an Eastern religion, but it has some of the larger religious populations in Asia. The religion is monotheistic and articulated by the Qur'an, which is a religious text considered by its adherents to be the verbatim word of their God *Allah*. It is the teachings of Muhammad, whom Muslims consider the last prophet of God. They believe that Islam is a primordial faith that was revealed many times before through prophets

---

[37] "Sikh", *Colliers Encyclopedia*, op. cit., p. 303

including Adam, Noah, Abraham, Moses, and Jesus. With about 1.7 billion followers or 23% of the global population, Islam is the second largest religion in the world. [38]

My youngest daughter became an exchange student and was assigned to live in Surabaya, Indonesia, with a Muslim family. Months later she returned, and her heritage as a Catholic served her well in a Muslim family. While not flaunting their religion, they are very devout. She returned to our Catholic home with great respect for the Islamic religious faith.

I have visited mosques in Europe, Africa, the Middle East, and Asia. A few years ago, I was invited to give a lecture as a "visiting scholar" at the Islamic Center of Greater Toledo, and I was graciously received there.

---

[38] Ibid

RELIGIOUS CULTURES
OF ASIAN NATIONS

As already mentioned, there is little commonality among Asian Religions.

CHINESE RELIGIOUS CULTURE:

China is not culturally monolithic because it covers vast regions through Tibet and Mongolia all the way to the South China Sea and north to the Sea of Japan, areas that contain many different religious and ethnic minorities. It is larger in area than the United States. The official governmental culture is atheist but China also contains many religious minorities. It is a country in transition from ancient rural cultures into the modern urban world and it is economically undergoing rapid growth as it grapples with the problems of unequal economic opportunity among its billion people.

Some Westerners think the Chinese are not religious, which is a misunderstanding; they have a long history of religious beliefs. The official position of the Chinese Communist Party is atheistic, but the government recognizes five religions: Buddhism, Taoism, Islam, Protestantism, and Catholicism (the Chinese Catholic Church and not the Roman Catholic Church.) [39]

---

[39] "Religion in China", Wikipedia, 2016

The Chinese people have been host to a variety of the most enduring philosophical traditions of the world, but these play only a minor role in modern China. Taoism, Confucianism, and Buddhism constitute the *three teachings* that have helped shape Chinese culture. Elements of these plus others are incorporated in folk religions.

Chinese folk religions are family-oriented and do not require exclusive adherence, allowing the practice of several; the term religion may be less descriptive than "cultural practices" as a more appropriate term with no clear boundary between religions. A kind of folk religion together with Taoism is practiced by some of the population, another small fraction is Buddhists, three percent are Christians, and two percent are Muslims. [40]

Christianity in China was introduced two times between the 7th and the 15th centuries, but failed to take root. Under Communism, foreign missionaries were expelled, most churches closed and their schools hospitals, and orphanages seized. During the Cultural Revolution, many priests were imprisoned. [41]

---

[40] Ibid
[41] Ibid

Despite a fragmented history of religion, it is obvious that a religious tendency still exists, but religion is a minor issue for most Chinese.

INDIA RELIGIOUS CULTURES:

The country of India is dominated by two religious cultures: Hindu and Sikh, neither of which is found outside of India.

Hindu religion: With approximately one billion followers, Hindu is the world's third largest religion (behind Christianity and Islam) and is the majority in India. Hinduism contains a broad range of philosophies with shared concepts and rituals. Scholars regard Hinduism as a synthesis of various Indian traditions. "Practices include rituals such as: worship, recitations, meditation, annual festivals, and occasional pilgrimages." [42]

Many Indians refer to Hinduism as Sanātana Dharma (the eternal law), which has a much deeper meaning than religion. All aspects of a Hindu life are part of dharma. From a Western standpoint it is referred to as a religion, but in India the term dharma

---

[42] "Hinduism", Wikipedia, 2016

is preferred, which is broader than the western term religion. [43]

SIKH religion. My first encounter with a Sikh was a fellow alumnus who was participating with me on a project for our alma mater, U.C. Berkeley. He was an electrical engineering graduate who worked as a scientist in Silicon Valley.

Understanding the essence of the Sikh of India is a challenge for Westerners. The polyglot nature of Sikhism makes it almost uncommunicable. The concept of God though theistic is mystical in character and the ideas concerning life after death are vague. "On the whole, Sikhism may be considered something racial, religious, or communal, or sometimes merely a movement." [44]

The Sikh religion arose in the 15th century at the time of the Mughal Empire. The Mughal emperors claimed direct descent from Genghis Khan, who ruled several centuries earlier.

The fundamental beliefs of Sikhism include faith and meditation in the name of the one creator and equality of all humankind. With over 25 million

---

[43] "Hindus in America", *Wikipedia,* op cit.

[44] "Sikh", *Colliers Encyclopedia,* op. cit., p. 303

adherents, Sikhism is one of the larger religions in Asia. [45]

RELIGIOUS CULTURE OF JAPAN:

Less than half of the population of Japan identifies with an organized religion: thirty percent are Buddhists, three percent are members of Shinto sects, and less than two percent are Christian. "The Japanese people are not particularly into religious philosophy." [46]

A majority of Japanese have some degree of syncretism with Buddhism. [47] They meditate and worship ancestors and gods at Shinto shrines but do not identify as Shinto in surveys because these religious terms have little meaning for the majority of the Japanese. The Japanese concept of "religion" is an invention of the 19th century. [48]

PAKISTANI RELIGIOUS CULTURE:

The state religion in Pakistan is Islam, which is practiced by about 98% of the people. The majority practice Sunni Islam with a small minority of Shias.

---

[45] "Sikhism", *Wikipedia*, 2016.

[46] "Religion in Japan", Wikipedia, 2016

[47] Syncretism: "The combination of different forms of belief or practice." op. cit., *Collegiate Dictionary*

[48] "Religion in Japan", Wikipedia, 2016

The constitution of Pakistan establishes Islam as the state religion. [49]

INDONESIA RELIGIOUS CULTURE:

I have a personal link with Indonesia when my youngest daughter was a teenage AFS exchange student living with an Islamic family in Surabaya. She found her Catholic religion very comfortable in living in a family Islamic environment. She has maintained close relationship with her three Indonesian sisters and a couple of them have visited her in America.

I also worked in Indonesia in the 1980's providing consulting services for modernization of a glass factory in Jakarta, and I was well received by the executives and hourly workforce there.

The history of Indonesia and its religion is shaped by geography, natural resources, wars, trade, economics, and politics. The nation is made of 6,000 inhabited islands that stretch along the equator in Southeast Asia. The islands are populated by peoples of various migrations, creating a diversity of cultures, ethnicities, and languages; however the major religious culture throughout Indonesia is Sunni Islam.

---

[49] "Religion in Pakistan", Wikipedia, 2016

IRANIAN RELIGIOUS CULTURE:

Iran is a theocracy that is guided by an Islamic ideology, which means that the God, Allah, is the source from which all authority derives. The 1979 constitution defines the political, economic, and social order and declares that Shi'a Islam is Iran's official religion.

ASSESSMENT OF ASIAN RELIGIONS:

As can be seen from an analysis of a few of the Asian religions, none of them believe in a monotheistic religion that is controlled by an almighty God such as in the Judeo-Christian and Islamic religions. That creates distinct differences between the Asian and European religious cultures.

ECONOMIES OF
ASIAN NATIONS

Now we turn to the matter of the economy and explore if the United States can successfully utilize economics and trade as it attempts to pivot to Asia. Certainly we can change our country's economic emphasis from Europe to Asia; that is not the issue. The question is if we can accomplish it in a manner that provides us with a dominate status in Asia. Let me repeat the point at issue: can we create a pivot toward Asia by establishing a towering role over the economies of Asian nations?

Having taken a brief look at religious philosophies in previous chapters, we recognize that economies are also influenced by the atheistic religious beliefs of the populations in Asia; hence, they have a much different State of Mind from our inherited European economic values.

How do you assess the economy of an Asian country; it is fraught with difficulty? For example, in the 1950's when Vietnam was at its end as a colony of France, how would you rate their economy - a country in Indo-China with mostly rice paddies and jungles? The United States, victorious in World War Two with the mightiest army in the world was determined that it would stop the spread of communism on the underside of Asia and accomplish it in Vietnam. During the following twenty years, the Presidents'

Eisenhower, Kennedy, Johnson, Nixon, and Ford all became involved in the effort. At the end of that twenty-year conflict, the United States was defeated and its rear-guard troops were rescued by helicopter from the roof of the American Embassy.

Oops, apparently we misjudged the economic viability of that impoverished Asian nation. Somehow we came up with the wrong assessment; where did we go wrong?

At the outset let us define "economics". It comes from the Greek meaning "management of a household". Adam Smith, a Scottish philosopher in 1776, originated the subject in his historic book, *Wealth of Nations.* [50] He connected the dots throughout a complex society and found many different social and economic aspects were interrelated to each other.

We discuss religion, politics, and economics separately but they are all interrelated; history is testimony to that. The religious state-of-mind in a country influences their attitude with regard to economics. An example of the underlying influence of religion on the economy includes the passive Hindu religious influence in India, or the aggressive atheistic

---

[50] Adam Smith, "An Inquiry into the Nature and Causes of the Wealth of Nations." 1777.

authority in China that influences economics in that nation.

A common way to measure the economy of a nation is to use metrics. If we can hang a number on a nation's economy, it seems to us to be better defined.

The following are countries ranked economically by GDP (gross national product) as measured by the IMF (International Monetary Fund).

RANK BY COUNTRY

BY NOMINAL BY GDP		GDP PER CAPITA
#1	UNITED STATES	5
2	CHINA	73
3	JAPAN	24
4	GERMANY	18
5	UNITED KINGDOM	25
7	INDIA	141
11	SOUTH KOREA	28
12	RUSSIA	48
13	AUSTRALIA	9
16	INDONESIA	116
18	TURKEY	63

22	TAWAIN	34
27	THAILAND	89
29	IRAN	96
38	SINGPORE	6
39	PHILLIPPINES	124
40	PAKISTAN	143
45	BANGLADESH	151
49	VIETNAM	132
55	N E W ZEALAND	21

There is a problem with the use of these metrics. They are mostly self-generated by the internal bureaucracy of a country, hence, reflect political numbers. Unfortunately, the bureaucrats are not above cooking-the-books to claim the most favorable numbers for their own country. For example: India's national bean counters are struggling to convince the world that their economy with idle factories, sagging exports and ailing banks grew by 7.5% in recent years and now appears to be the world's fastest-growing economy, outpacing China. "But skepticism about the data is growing fast." [51] As we utilize statistics, we must remember metrics are only man-made numbers and not infallible.

---

[51] "The Elephant in the stats", *The Economist*", April 9th 2016, p. 73

World-wide economics started in Asia with trade. Vasco da Gama was a Portuguese explorer and the first European to reach India by sea, linking Europe and Asia and the Indian Ocean with the Orient. This was accomplished in 1497 AD, only five years after the Spanish discovery of America by Columbus. The world became connected and international trade became the new kid-on-the-block. Vasco Da Gama's discovery of the sea route to India opened the way for an age of global imperialism and for European countries to establish their colonial empires in Asia.

It would be another three hundred years after Vasco Da Gama before the term, economics, was introduced by the Scottish Adam Smith in his treatise *Wealth of Nations*. Published in 1776, the book provided one of the first descriptions of the things that build a nations' wealth and it is still today a classic in economics. [52]

But, there is vulnerability in the use of certain terminology from one culture and applying it in another. It compares apples and oranges. Adam Smith was a Scotsman and his economics is a theory from Western civilization; hence, may not be valid as a concept in Asia because a rice paddy and jungle hut in Vietnam is not the same as a software company

---

[52] Adam Smith, *An Inquiry into the Nature and Cause of the Wealth of Nations*, 1776

in Silicon Valley. How does China, formerly with rice paddy farmers in a rural landscape, measure its economy today when the majorities of Chinese have moved to the cities and engage in a completely different line of work: manufacturing? What metric is appropriate?

As a nation, we are faced with a dilemma in characterizing the economic resources of Asia as we consider how to pivot our policies to react to threats or opportunities from that direction, bearing in mind our lack of success in the Asian wars we have fought during this century.

We will utilize economic statistics as we analyze Asian nations, but admit we don't know how to factor in the two most important resources in many countries: people and leadership. We learned that lesson in Vietnam.

Looking at the GDP chart, how do we interpret it?

The economy of the United States, which is 1st, has the greatest impact on the world's economy. China's economy is 2nd, Japan's 3rd, and Germany's is 4th. How do the people within these countries perceive their economy as it impacts on their own standard-of-living? Do they see it the same as we do? We can only guess at the perception of the people toward their own situation, since we do not really know how they feel. Japan's ranks 24th, Russia ranks 48th, and China's ranks 73; and we question if these numbers are true measures of the feeling of the people involved toward their own lives. Putin who runs Russia, which is ranked 48th, has an approval rating with his own people well above 50%, a level any U.S. President would be happy to receive.

Standard-of-living refers to the level of wealth, comfort, material goods and necessities available to people. The standard-of-living is closely related to quality-of-life – or is it?[53]

The total population of the world is 7.4 billion people with over half of them in Asia. As we consider the large differences in economic metrics, it suggests that even GDP per capita may be a poor indicator of economic resources. We can look at these metric numbers, but they are problematic. As mentioned earlier, they arise internally within a country, hence, are subject to cooking-the-books. As a consequence of this, we also need a subjective look at realities in each nation to appraise the true economic health of Asian nations. Here are subjective descriptions for the three largest economies.

---

[53] "Standard of Living", Wikipedia, 2016

CHINESE ECONOMIC CULTURE:

China is a cradle of civilization with a history beginning with an ancient people that flourished in the basin of the Yellow River. In the 18th century, Adam Smith, [54] claimed that China had long been one of the most fertile, best cultivated, most industrious, most prosperous, and most urbanized country with the largest economy in the world for much of the past two thousand years. [55]

Starting in the 1930's, a downturn occurred. The Chinese economy was heavily disrupted by the war against Japan from 1937 to 1949. Following the war, the economy of China became dominated by a communistic government. The purges of the Cultural Revolution under Mao Zedong further disrupted the economy. [56]

After Mao Zedong's death, economic reforms began when Deng Xiaoping ousted the Maoist faction in 1978. Reforms were carried out in two stages: collectivization of agriculture was dropped, and some state-owned industries became private. The private

---

[54] Adam Smith, op. cit.
[55] "Chinese Economic Reform", Wikipedia, 2016
[56] Ibid

sector grew rapidly, accounting for as much as 70% of GDP by 2005. [57]

China has now become one of the world's most powerful economies. Already its socialist economy is the second largest by GDP; however, in the chart of GDP per capita it ranks only 84th because of its huge population. [58]

There is a concern with China's year-over-year GDP growth. The economic statistics represent the results starting from a very low base so the level of improvement is misleading; also, the Chinese people are in potential turmoil as a result of income inequality. Their leaders are in jeopardy of losing control; they went through a revolution in 1950, and it could happen again. Even though China is communistic, it does have a business cycle, and is currently undergoing a recession.

I have been to China several times and was the Shore Patrol Officer pressed into duty in Hong Kong when a U.S. aircraft carrier arrived in port with its many thousands of sailors all intent on going to bars and having a good time. Assigned as a member of a convoy of British Police, I was told to keep my naval officer uniform and presence visible, which was all

[57] "Chinese Economic Reform", Wikipedia, 2015
[58] "Economy of China", Wikipedia, 2016

they wanted from me; however, I did get an epic guided tour of all the hot spots of Hong Kong. At that point in my naval career, I had seen more than enough of the Asian landscape and populations. Little did I know I still had Indonesia, Malaysia, Singapore, Taiwan, and a lot more of Japan in my future?

ECONOMIC CULTURE OF INDIA:

The strong traditions of the Hindu and Sikh religious culture had a profound impact that enabled the people of India to survive a century of brutal subjugation by the British Empire and emerge to become one of the economic powerhouses of the 21st century.

Ancient India showed promise before colonization by the British Empire in the nineteenth century took a toll. The British occupation ended in 1947 and the impact of this on India's economy is a controversial topic. The Indian economy has been characterized by pervasive corruption and slow growth.

The Economy of India is now the seventh-largest in the world measured by overall GDP, but ranked 122 by GDP per Capita. The long-term growth prospective of the Indian economy is positive due to its young population; however, the politics and economy of India have been an enigma to many. Why has social progress been so slow? Does this reflect, perhaps, a passive mindset that comes from the Hindu tradition and mindset?

With 1.2 billion people, India's recent progress has been impressive. It has one of fastest growing service sectors in the world with a large educated English-speaking population. It has become a major exporter of information technology services and software services and is also the fourth largest start-up hub in the world with over 3,100 technology start-ups in 2015; however, economic growth isn't yet generating enough jobs for the million people who enter India's workforce each month. [59]

ECONOMIC CULTURE OF JAPAN:

The economy of Japan is the third-largest in the world. According to the International Monetary Fund, the country's per capita GDP (PPP) was the 28th highest in 2014.

Japan is the world's third largest automobile manufacturing country, has the largest electronics goods industry, and is often ranked among the world's most innovative countries leading several measures of global patent filings. Facing increasing competition

[59] "India's success is built to last", *Time*, July, 1016

from China and South Korea, manufacturing in Japan today now focuses primarily on high-tech and precision goods, such as optical instruments, hybrid vehicles, and robotics.

In the three decades of economic development following 1960, Japan ignored defense spending in favor of economic growth, thus allowing for a rapid economic growth referred to as the Japanese post-war economic miracle. Japan was able to establish and maintain itself as the world's second largest economy from 1978 until 2010, when it was surpassed by the People's Republic of China. [60]

---

[60] IBID

AN ASIAN ECONOMIC
PIVOT?

A pivot to Asia by the U.S. will be difficult to accomplish because we have never had much leverage over Asian economies. No country in Asia is a principle trading partner compared to our neighbors, Mexico and Canada, or countries in Europe; hence, we have little clout in Asia.

Another issue is the Golden Rule. The Christian religious philosophies of the U.S. population differ from those of Asia in the implementation of the Golden Rule. We give considerable credibility to that religious tenet in our economic dealing, but it is meaningless to an atheist in Asia.

The Golden Rule is a precept of altruism seen in many human religions and cultures and a unilateral moral commitment among Christians to the well-being of others without expecting anything in return. We express the Golden Rule in America (or the law of reciprocity as it is called by non-Christians) as the requirement to treat others as one would wish to be treated.

The Golden Rule, which exists in many religions and ethical traditions, can be explained from the perspectives of psychology, philosophy, sociology, and human evolution, but it has little influence in Asian economics. Philosophers suggest that in economics without some kind of reciprocity, a society would lack the incentive for bartering or making trade deals. Absent this motivation, there would be a huge penalty to economic relationships; hence, our lack of leverage in the economies of Asia.

The first modern Christian references of to the Golden Rule occurred in the early 17th century in Britain by Anglican theologians and preachers. This was before Adam Smith called attention in his book, *Wealth of Nations* to the complex interrelationships among all elements of society. [61]

Long before the origin of Christianity, the Golden Rule existed among the major philosophical schools of ancient China: Monism, Taoism, and Confucianism. The interpretation by Confucius was to never impose on others "what you would not choose for yourself." The Golden Rule even extends further back in time into ancient China, suggesting if people regarded other people's families in the same way that they regard their own, who then would incite their own family to attack that of another?

The variations in the meaning of the Golden Rule are reflected in differing approaches to economic philosophy, particularly in the modern era of international trade. For most Asian nations, reciprocity as reflected in the Golden Rule is approached as a

[61] Adam Smith, Op. Cit.

pragmatic matter of negotiation to be decided during the bartering and implementation of trade deals. Atheistic Asian nations are willing to follow the letter of the Golden Rule, but lose sight of the intent. As a Christian nation, we look outward to an Almighty God in implementing the Golden Rule; whereas, the approach in Asia is to look inward in a pragmatic and non-secular way to get the best possible deal for their country.

The globalization concept now in vogue has saddled the United States with an additional penalty. The metaphor of a level playing field places a restraint on our religious ethics, but Asians are not similarly constrained. We worry about a moral code; Asians do not.

In addition to the issues involving religion, there is also the matter of geography and history. Asian nations are far removed half-way around the world from the United States with many intervening miles that have always discouraged strong trade relationships.

Is it possible to utilize economics in a successful pivot toward Asia? The answer is: probably not. We have little leverage and virtually no control over the economies of Asia.

POLITICS IN ASIAN
NATIONS

We turn now to a consideration of politics. They are also altered by the religious beliefs of a population. Is it likely that the U.S. can create a successful political pivot with the nations of Asia and gain domination over political affairs?

In Asia, politics is not for the faint-hearted. Within this century, Asians suffered four man-made catastrophes in addition to the Vietnam and Afghanistan Wars: China went through the Cultural Revolution; Bangladesh was born amid mass slaughter; Cambodia's Khmers Rouges inflicted genocide on their own countrymen; and Indonesia's army killed hundreds of thousands as General Suharto consolidated his 32-year dictatorship.

Here are a few observations about politics in Asia:

* Countries place emphasis on having a constitution.
* Despite constitutions, several governments changed by coup d'état, assassination, or are governed by military junta.
* Several Asian nations are ruled by a de-facto dictator.
* Countries will change their political affiliation for local issues, or a tactic for trade negotiations.

* During the past century, nearly one-half the nations of Asia have changed or reversed their political leaning with respect to the United States.
* Definitions of communism and socialism as economic realities are no longer valid.

It is challenging to remain objective where censorship and repression are common; hence, difficult to remain factual and objective in the muddied waters of some regimes. Here are the political profiles of several Asian nations.

CHINESE POLITICAL CULTURE:

When it comes to political organizations in Asia, the elephant-in-the-room is the Chinese Communist Party.

The history of early China was chaotic with many regions ruled by local warlords. A power struggle ensued during the 1930's between the Nationalist leader Chiang Kai-shek and communist Mao Zedong. The latter won the conflict and in the 1950's Chiang Kai-shek and his army fled to the Chinese island of Taiwan.

Following the death of Mao in 1976, a political struggle erupted. Deng Xiaoping won and became the Paramount Leader. He introduced the concept of socialism, which generated significant economic growth that still continues to this day. [62]

The highest body of the Chinese Communist Party is the National Congress, convened every fifth year. The party leader holds the offices of General Secretary, Chairman of Military Affairs, and State President. The current party leader is Xi Jinping, who was elected at the 18th National Congress held in 2012.

The Chinese Communist Party has 88 million with the following membership: [63]

25.8 μ (million): farmers, and herdsmen.

21.7 μ: women.

12.5 μ: managing, professional, and technical.

9.0 μ: administrative staff.

7.4 μ: party cadres.

7.3 μ: workers

Contrary to Xi Jinping's wishes, capitalism has blossomed under the Chinese Communist Party. The country now has 200 billionaires, which puts the

---

[62] "Chinese Communist Party", Wikipedia, 2016

[63] Ibid

country second in the world after the United States. [64] Is it any wonder that there is a serious problem of income inequality within China?

TAIWAN POLITICS:

My first experience with Taiwan was in 1951 when my destroyer pulled into Keelung, Taiwan, shortly thereafter on a visit to show the support of the United States for Chiang Kai-shek. Keelung was an absolute chaotic hell-hole with Nationalist forces living in the streets after chasing the Taiwanese natives into the hills. Our ship was on a "show the flag" mission. I went ashore in a rickshaw to their Army Officer Club that was a one-room dilapidated shack. I sat at a table with five Taiwan Major Generals, none of whom was yet in their thirties.

In the sixty-five years since then, the Taiwan Government has become a major international power, but the Chinese

Government still considers Taiwan as an island of China and has vowed to get it back. After six decades, Taiwan remains a festering political wound in Asia.

INDIA POLITICS:

---

[64] "Billionaires in China", Wikipedia, 2016

India was ruled as a colony of the British Empire and gained independence in 1947. The British virtually abandoned India. The provinces were partitioned into the two new countries of India and Pakistan with Bangladesh evolving later. [65]

It was a brutal breakup as the intermixed Muslims, Sikhs, and Hindus had to move to new areas: Muslims to Pakistan, and Hindus and Sikhs to India. Political and ethnic scars remain and India and Pakistan have been on the verge of warfare since, including two border wars. That is particularly worrisome inasmuch as both countries are now armed with nuclear bombs.

The government is formed through elections held every five years. India had its first general election in 1951. The election of 2014 established single-party rule in the country with the BJP (Bharatiya Janata Party). The BJP Party had 100 million registered members as of April 2015 and is the largest political party in Asia. [66]

Poverty, unemployment, and caste-related violence are issues that influence politics. In 1991 the former Prime Minister Rajiv Gandhi was assassinated during an election campaign.

---

[65] "History of India", Wikipedia, 2016
[66] ibid

Law and order are treated as minor issues during elections. Many elected legislators have criminal cases against them. In July 2008, the *Washington Post* reported that nearly a fourth of the 540 Indian Parliament members faced criminal charges, "including human trafficking, immigration rackets, embezzlement, rape and murder". [67]

In India there are 110 billionaires; the 100 richest people in India hold 2/3 of the wealth of the population, which has led to severe economic inequality. [68]

During the past fifty years, India has never maintained a long-term stable political relationship with its neighbors or with the United States.

POLITICAL CULTURE OF JAPAN:

Human habitation in the Japanese archipelago can be traced to prehistoric times. By the eighth century AD, Japan's many kingdoms and tribes gradually came to be unified under an Emperor, and the imperial dynasty established at that time still continues to this day.

The Japanese military invaded Manchuria in 1931 and the conflict escalated into a prolonged war with

---

[67] ibid

[68] Forbes list of Indian Billionaires.

China. Japan's attack on Pearl Harbor in December 1941 led to war with the United States and its allies. Japan's unconditional surrender in 1945 followed the atomic bombing and destruction of the cities Hiroshima and Nagasaki. The Allies occupied Japan from the end of the war until 1952. A new constitution was enacted in 1947 that transformed Japan into a parliamentary monarchy. [69]

At the time of Japanese independence, I was on my third tour in the Korean War and a frequent visitor of ports in Japan where my destroyer returned for supplies and fuel. Travelling extensively throughout Japan, I learned a bit of conversational Japanese and felt welcomed everywhere. The American occupation was conducted with no American military personnel carrying arms, which created a mutual spirit of friendliness.

The politics of Japan are conducted in a multi-party constitutional monarchy whereby the Emperor acts as the ceremonial head of state and the Prime Minister is the head of government. Legislative power is vested in the National Diet, which consists of the House of Representatives and the House of Councilors. Judicial power is vested in the Supreme Court. [70]

---

[69] "History of Japan", Wikipedia, 2016

[70] "Politics of Japan", Wikipedia, 2016

The chief of the executive branch, the Prime Minister, is a member of the Diet and must be a civilian. With the Liberal Democratic Party (LDP) in power, it has been convention that the President of the party serves as the Prime Minister. Several political parties exist in Japan, but the Liberal Democratic Party has dominated for 70 years since the war. [71]

Japan has been one of our strongest allies in Asia since the end of World War Two. I personally have the highest respect and feeling of friendship for the government of Japan and the Japanese people.

POLITICS IN PAKISTAN

This subject was previously mentioned but will be partially repeated here because of its importance in Asia.

India was ruled as a colony of the British Empire and gained independence in 1947. The provinces were then partitioned into the two new countries of India and Pakistan with Bangladesh evolving later. [72]

It was a brutal breakup as the intermixed Muslims, Sikhs, and Hindus had to move to new areas: Muslims to Pakistan, and Hindus and Sikhs to India. Political

---

[71] Ibid

[72] "History of India", Wikipedia, 2016

and ethnic scars still remain and India and Pakistan have been on the verge of warfare since, including two border wars. That is particularly worrisome inasmuch as both countries are now armed with nuclear bombs.

VIETNAM:

I gained an unusual perspective of Vietnam with a friendship with my namesake, Larry Keating, a well know international war correspondent. I met him in the Hong Kong Foreign Correspondents Club that had invited our ship to utilize it as our officer's club. He was sitting in front of a Victorian fireplace with a huge dog at his feet, and he welcomed the intrusion of an American naval officer. He had been tramping and reporting for several years on the war going on in the French colony of Vietnam. We discussed it at length. This was a few weeks before the battle of Dien Bien Phu, when the French were defeated and driven out.

It is difficult to understand how the United States a few weeks later became involved in the far-away jungles of Vietnam; the war was a disaster.

The history of Vietnam can be traced back 4000 years. Ancient Vietnam was home to some of the world's earliest civilizations and one of the world's first people who practiced agriculture. Once Vietnam succumbed to foreign rule it proved unable to escape from it for a thousand years; Vietnam was successively governed by a series of Chinese dynasties; then as a French colony. [73]

In September 1945, Ho Chi Minh proclaimed the Democratic Republic of Vietnam with fighting between the Viet Minh and France. The United States got sucked into the war by supplying a few "advisors" authorized by President Eisenhower; it escalated under the new naïve President Kennedy.

In the aftermath of the Vietnam War (1954–75), the Viet Cong unified the country under communist rule. The war left Vietnam devastated with a total death toll estimated at between 800,000 and 3.1 million and many thousands more crippled by weapons and substances dropped from American planes. The losses of American troops and cost of the Vietnam War to the United States was a disaster and our nation still carries the scars of that war.

Now, fifty years later, Vietnam is a Socialist Republic with a one-party system led by the Communist Party of Vietnam (CPV). Sharing a border with China, the two nations are somewhat adversaries. It is thought that the country is a bulwark against a southern Asian

---

[73] "History of Vietnam", Wikipedia, 2016

aggression by China; hence, the U.S. is openly courting the current communistic regime of Vietnam.

Despite control by a communist government, even Vietnam has a billionaire. The most likely candidate for the second billionaire is a businessman in rubber plantations, hydropower, real estate, and a soccer club. Even communists governments tolerate billionaires. [74]

INDONESIAN POLITICS:

The Portuguese Vasco De Gama linked Europe to Indonesia with his explorations in 1497. Other Europeans arrived during the 16th century with the Dutch becoming the dominant power. The Japanese invasion in 1942 and subsequent occupation during the World War Two ended Dutch rule. Two days after the surrender of Japan, nationalist leader, Sukarno, declared independence and became the first president of Indonesia.

After a chaotic period, Sukarno established an autocratic system with support of the Indonesian Communist Party. He became a virtual dictator and embarked policies with aid from the Soviet Union and Communist China. In the 1960s, the economy deteriorated drastically as a result of political

---

[74] "How many Billionaires in Vietnam", Wikipedia, 2016

instability and by the time of Sukarno's downfall the economy was in chaos with 1,000% annual inflation, shrinking export revenues, crumbling infrastructure, factories operating at minimal capacity, and negligible investment.

Sukarno was replaced in 1967 by one of his generals, Suharto, and remained under house arrest until his death. The new President brought discipline to economic policy, reduced inflation, stabilized the currency, and attracted foreign investment. [75]

During the regime of President Suharto, Indonesia built strong relations with the United States. Indonesia is a founding member of the Association of South East Asian Nations (ASEAN), and has worked to develop close political and economic ties with its neighbors. The government has co-operated with the United States on tracking Islamic fundamentalism and terrorist groups. Indonesia currently is one of our strongest allies in Asia. [76]

SOUTH KOREA:

I was involved in the history of South Korea and wear a citation from President Syngmam Rhee awarded

---

[75] "History of Indonesia", Wikipedia, 2016
[76] Ibid

for my ship's role in fighting up and down the North Korean coast. Leading a shore patrol team, I also a spent a brief time embedded with South Korean army forces on our occupied island of Yodo inside the North Korean Wonsan Harbor.

The history of South Korea began after the end of World War Two when President Rhee officially declared independence. In the aftermath of the Japanese occupation which ended in 1945, Korea was divided at the 38 parallel by a United Nations resolution to be administered by the Soviet Union in the north and the United States in the south. They were unable to agree on Joint Trusteeship over Korea. This led in 1948 to the establishment of two governments, each claiming to be the legitimate government of all of Korea. Following the Korean War, the two governments became North and South Korea. [77]

In 2004, the Assembly voted to impeach the president and the Prime Minister became an Acting President. The Constitutional Court overturned the impeachment and Roh was reinstated. [78] In 2017 the South Korean President was again impeached and removed with the Vice President assuming control – what happens next?

---

[77] "History of South Korea", Wikipedia, 2016
[78] "Politics in South Korea", Wikipedia, 2016

In 1950, North Korea suddenly launched a massive assault on South Korea and seized virtually the entire country. President Truman immediately ordered the American Military to repulse the attack, which was labeled as a United Nations Police Action. North Korea overran virtually the entire peninsula. The American forces launched a surprise amphibious operation that caught North Korean forces in an exposed position and they retreated all the way to their northern border along the Yalu River. At that point the American Army suddenly faced hordes of Chinese soldiers crossing the Yalu and coming down on them. After several years of fighting, the conflict became a stalemate near the 38th parallel. An armistice was signed to cease hostilities, and that remains the situation now 60 years later. Technically, we still remain in a "state of war" with North Korea.

South Korea has risen from one of the poorest countries in the world and devastation in 1950 when it was overrun by North Korean forces to become one of the economic powerhouses of Asia.

South Korea is not a bulwark of stable government. The current president has recently been impeached and removed from office, the second time this has happened within a decade. A newly elected President is now on the scene.

AUSTRALIA:

Australia is somewhat like having a slice of America "down under". After the American Revolution when England was no longer able to use the Carolinas and Georgia as a dumping ground for prisoners, it began to disembark prisoners in the newly discovered Australia near present day Sydney. [79]

During my O-I career, I provided consulting services to our Australian affiliate over period of several years. They had a glass factory in every major city and I worked in all six of them. I developed the highest regard and friendship for the government and people of Australia.

Inasmuch as we should never take the loyalty and support of any other government for granted, it is accurate to say that Australia has been one of America's staunchest allies for a century.

IRANIAN POLITICS:

Iran has an elected president, parliament, Guardian Council (which elects the Supreme Leader), and local councils. All candidates running for these positions must be vetted by the Guardian Council before being

---

[79] Robert Hughes, *The Fatal Shore*, Alfred,A Knopf, New York, 1987

elected. The Supreme Leader appoints the Guardian Council.

The early days of the Iranian revolutionary government were characterized by political tumult. In November 1979 the American embassy was seized and its occupants taken hostage and kept captive for 444 days because of prior American Government support for the Shah of Iran.

An eight-year war between Iran and Iraq killed hundreds of thousands and cost the country billions of dollars. By mid-1982, a succession of power struggles left the revolutionary leader Ayatollah Khomeini and his supporters in power.

The most powerful political office in Iran is the Supreme Leader, the founder of the Islamic Republic, Ayatollah Khomeini, and his successor, Ayatollah Ali Khamenei. The Supreme leader is the Head of State and can veto the laws made by parliament. Iran is in essence a dictatorship under the control of the Supreme Leader.

NORTH KOREA:

North Korea has been ruled by a family succession of dictators after it was liberated from the Japanese at the end of World War Two; Kim II-sung became the ruler in 1948 and was replaced by his son and grandson. In practice, North Korea functions as a one-party state under a totalitarian family dictatorship, described as an absolute monarchy with Kim Il-sung and his heirs as its rulers.

Despite the constitution's provisions for democracy, the present Supreme Leader, Kim Jong-un (grandson of the state's founder, Kim Il-sung), exercises absolute control over the government and the country. The ruling party is the Workers' Party of Korea (WPK). The WPK has been in power since its creation in 1948.

While the North Korean constitution formally guarantees protection of human rights, in practice there are severe limits on freedom of expression, and the government closely supervises the lives of North Korean citizens. [80]

In May 2016, Kim convened a congress of the Worker's Party of Korea, which was the first formal gathering of the party in more than three decades. Because of censorship, little is known about the proceedings.

The erratic leadership of North Korea is a concern of all its neighbors. It now has several nuclear bombs and is rapidly building the missal capability to deliver them to the western United States. The nation is an

---

[80] "Politics of North Korea", Wikipedia, 2016

enigma for which there is presently no military option or a realistic solution.

Returning now to the initial question: can the U.S. create a political pivot with the nations of Asia? History is not on our side. We have experienced a mixed bag of support from major nations in Asia, and we have little leverage over their political fortunes.

IS A POLITICAL PIVOT
TO ASIA POSSIBLE?

There are difficulties for the U.S in executing the current potential pivot in the politics of Asia.

There is an exception to prove -the -rule. At the end of World War Two, the armed forces of the U.S. had saved Asia from the Japanese. Our forces had achieved domination of virtually all Asian territories and we had achieved a pivot to Asia – maybe. Need we go through the entire scenario, which is well known? Then began the post-war U.S. excursions of political power, first the Korean War that produced a stalemate that led to an armistice and we are still technically in a state-of-war with North Korea. Then shortly followed the fourteen-year war with Vietnam where we were defeated. We no longer were a dominate force in Asia and un-pivoted with our tail between our legs back to dealing with issues of Europe and the Middle East. A successful pivot is difficult to establish and maintain. Political leverage is the use of influence or power to achieve dominance. We currently lack any political leverage of consequence over Asian nations.

The politics of Asia are varied as would be expected of such a large landmass with a diverse population and many different forms of government: monarchies, one-party states, federal states, dependent territories, liberal democracies, and military dictatorships. Politics and economics have a long history throughout right from the start after the ancient voyage of Vasco Da Gama. Much of the political climate in Asia today is still affected by colonialism and imperialism of the past with some states retaining close links with their former colonial governors while others involved in bitter struggles, the consequences of which continue to be felt. [81]

The situation today remains jumbled. There continue to be hostilities in parts of Asia, primarily between India and Pakistan, as well as economic competitiveness between the People's Republic of China and India. China and India do not have a peace treaty, nor does Russia with Japan or North Korea with South Korea. Our relations with China alternate between hot and cold.

Is it possible to achieve an Asian political pivot? That is unlikely; we currently have little leverage among Asian nations with such diverse and unrelated interests. When the foreign policy of the United States pivots in one direction, there is usually an adversarial nation that reacts in the opposite way.

The sixty-year policy of containment of communism by western governments finds Russia as its focus; China has been the beneficiary of that policy. When Nixon went to China it was to jerk Russia, not a new-found

---

[81] "Politics in Asia", Wikipedia 2017

love for things Chinese. Now with the administration of Trump calling the shots, he alternately holds China in an embrace or at arms-length in a reactive policy of looking for leverage in Asia.

We recently invited the Head of State of India, Modi, to a State Dinner at the White House, a rare honor, in an attempt to develop closer ties with India as part of our pivot. Yet it has shown little effect and the passive and ambivalent policies of India remain unchanged.

We have now announced that the several decade-long strategy of dealing with North Korea has been a failure. We attempt to utilize a relationship with China in having them lean on North Korea, which is their major trading partner, to bring North Korea into a family of nations. That has failed and we ponder why? Is it for lack of trying or for lack of any real leverage over North Korea by China?

Some other Asian nations have alternately been friends or political foes, depending on their national interest at the time. That included Indonesia, now a strong friend; Vietnam, who sees us as a buffer with China; Pakistan, who waffles back and forth; the Philippines, who currently have an anti-American President who is seeking political handouts; and South Korea who recently impeached their president and removed her from office and is swinging in the Asian wind.

Returning now to the initial question: can the U.S. create a political pivot with the nations of Asia? History is not on our side. We have experienced a mixed bag of support from major nations in Asia, and we have little leverage over their political fortunes. The likelihood of achieving a pivot within such a menagerie of diverse motivations of national interests is dim.

SUMMARY AND CONCLUSIONS

1. The Pivot to Asia was a new Foreign Affairs policy of the United States announced by President Obama in 2014 that places greater emphasis on economic and political matters in Asia. It remains to be seen if it is to be a policy in the Trump Administration.

2. We have done an inadequate job of relating to Asian nations in the recent past and future prospects are questionable. We have fought unsuccessful wars in Korea and Vietnam and squandered the political capital earned from World War Two.

3. The religious belief in a monotheistic God of the Judeo- Christian and Islamic religions are a major difference between the United States and the atheistic religious beliefs of Asian nations.

4. Religious beliefs affect the state-of-mind and priorities of governments for economic and political issues; hence, a major difference with Asia for these matters. The Judeo- Christian religious faith in the United States requires a role for Christian mores, but there is no similar requirement among the atheistic nations of Asia; therefore, we have differing social philosophies.

5. An actual pivot in foreign policy requires the use of leverage to create a dominating role.

Absent such clout, accomplishing an actual pivot is unlikely. *Economics*: the United States has been unable to establish economic leverage over Asian nations.

6. Politics: the United States has been unable to establish political leverage over Asian nations, which is sufficient to demonstrate dominance.

7. A major hurdle for the United States is due to its religious belief in an almighty God coupled with ignorance and lack of acceptance of the Asian atheistic religions.

8. Therefore; the new Foreign Affairs policy of a Pivot to Asia by the United States is unlikely to be fruitful. Although we can change our internal emphasis from Europe and Middle East matters to those of Asia, the reality is that success is: "not likely."

APPENDICE: UNITED STATES FOREIGN POLICY

During the years that followed the breakup of the Soviet Union, the United States took on the character of international policeman; the United States became involved in military conflicts around the globe. "Police action" is a euphemism for a military action undertaken without a formal declaration of war. Here is a list of police actions undertaken by the United States after the end of our last declared war – World War Two:

> Korean War, 1950-53. (U. N. police action)
> Vietnam War, 1955-75.
>
> Soviet War in Afghanistan, 1979-89 (resistance of Taliban paid for by U.S. CIA).
>
> Marines go to Lebanon, 1982.
>
> Invasion of Grenada, 1982.
>
> Invasion of Panama, 1989.
>
> 1st Gulf War, 1991.

Somalia, 1993.

The Balkans: Yugoslavia, Bosnia, Kosovo, 1994.

Haiti uprising, 1994.

Bombing campaign in Kosovo, 1999.

Afghanistan War, 2001-2017, ongoing.

Iraq no-fly zone, 2002.

Iraq War, 2003- 2017, ongoing.

Libya revolution, 2011.

Syrian Civil War, 2013 – 2017, ongoing.

Special Forces against ISIL, 2016 – 2017, ongoing.

Where will we fight the next police action? It will most likely be in Asia since we still maintain a force of American army troops in South Korea as a defensive deterrent to North Korea, and a military force in Japan and in Okinawa as we did sixty five years ago. The United States still maintains the same naval bases in Yokosuka and Sasebo, Japan, where my destroyer returned for supplies after bombarding the North Korean shore installations. Little has changed militarily in Asia during the past six decades. A tentative peace remains fragile.

A geopolitical pivot to Asia is a complex undertaking. Let's face reality. We have few adequate bases of operations on the Asian continent and are able to maintain naval bases only in friendly nations such as Japan, Okinawa, South Korea, the Philippines, and Taiwan. None of these are adequate offensively or defensively. We learned that lesson during the Korean War when hordes of Chinese troops crossed the Yalu River into Korea overwhelming American forces and we settled for an armistice on the Korean peninsula that, sixty years later, still remains fragile with our two nations technically in a state-of-war.

Superimposed on this is the world-wide scourge of nuclear weapons. Of the nine countries in the world known to have nuclear bombs, four of them are in Asia: China (with 260 nuclear bombs), Pakistan (130), India (120), and North Korea (<10); at the same time, Europe is not without concern: Russia has 7300 nuclear bombs, United Kingdom with 215, France with 300, and Israel with 80. The United States has 6970. [82]

Our world is fraught with potential calamities, and there is a concern that conflicts in Asia are likely to play a huge role in the future. We cannot disengage from Europe, but countries in Asia are increasingly "eating our lunch."

---

[82] USA TODAY 3/30/2016

www.ingramcontent.com/pod-product-compliance
Lightning Source LLC
Chambersburg PA
CBHW050400290526
45786CB00003B/1066